1 9 8 7
The Year You Were Born

Birth Certificate

Name: _____

Birthdate: _____

Time: _____

Place of Birth: _____

Weight: _____ Length: _____

Mother's maiden name: _____

Father's name: _____

To Caroline and Kelly Martinet from Auntie Jeanne J.M.

To Jacob William Prescott Carroll and Jake Gauthier J.L.

Inquiries should be addressed to Tambourine Books,
a division of William Morrow & Company, Inc.,
1350 Avenue of the Americas, New York, New York 10019.
Printed in the United States of America

ISBN 0-688-11970-0 (pbk.) ISBN 0-688-11971-9 (lib.)

1 3 5 7 9 10 8 6 4 2
First edition

1987
The Year You Were Born

Compiled by

JEANNE MARTINET

Illustrated by

JUDY LANFREDI

Tambourine Books  New York

U.S. Almanac
1987

International Year of Shelter for the Homeless

The Year of the Reader

World population
5,024,000,000

United States population
243,915,000
Males 118,987,000
Females 124,928,000

Number of births in the U.S.
3,809,000
Boys 1,951,000
Girls 1,858,000

Average length at birth 20 inches

Average weight at birth 7 pounds, 7 ounces

Deaths in the U.S.
2,123,000

Size of the U.S.
3,618,770 square miles

President
Ronald Reagan

Biggest state (in area)
Alaska, 591,004 square miles

Longest river
Mississippi-Missouri, 3,710 miles

Tornadoes 656

Households with TV sets
87,000,000

Households with VCRs
43,000,000

Top crop
Corn

Total 1987 output
181,000,000 metric tons

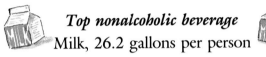

Top nonalcoholic beverage
Milk, 26.2 gallons per person

Children's books sold
220,000,000

Boy Scouts 4,180,000
Girl Scouts 2,274,000

Most popular girl's name Jessica
Most popular boy's name Matthew

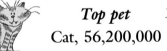

Top pet
Cat, 56,200,000

Most popular hat
The baseball cap, 300,000,000 sold

Number of daily newspapers published
1,645

Number of icebergs in the world
320,000

January

*J*anuary is named after Janus, the Roman god
of doorways and of beginnings.

BIRTHSTONE *Garnet*

THURSDAY
January 1

New Year's Day • Bolivia issues a new form of money called
the *boliviano;* it's equal to 1,000,000 of the old pesos.

FRIDAY
January 2

A new type of cockroach has been discovered in Florida: the
Asian cockroach, which reproduces quickly and can fly long
distances. 100,000 of them have been reported in some areas.

SATURDAY
January 3

2 Coast Guard boats rescue 31 passengers
from a capsized cruise catamaran that ran
aground on a reef near Honolulu, Hawaii.

SUNDAY
January 4

DISASTER: In the worst Amtrak accident in history, a
passenger train crashes into 3 diesel locomotives northeast
of Baltimore, Maryland.

MONDAY
January 5

President Ronald Reagan has minor surgery at
the Bethesda Navy Medical Center in Maryland.

TUESDAY
January 6

NEWBORN GALAXY: Astronomers at the University of California
announce the birth of a brand-new, giant galaxy. It contains
about 1 billion stars and is very far away—12 billion light-
years from earth.

WEDNESDAY
January 7

The nuclear reactor in Richland, Washington, which makes
plutonium for the U.S. arsenal, shuts down to make
$50,000,000 worth of safety improvements.

THURSDAY
January 8

Police officers in Indio, California, pull over a
stolen bakery truck after chasing it for 4 miles.
The driver and the cops fight it out—
by throwing pies at each other!

FRIDAY
January 9

Joe Mizelle, Jr., sets a fishing record by catching a 9-pound,
8-ounce black sea bass in Virginia Beach, Virginia.

WHO ELSE WAS BORN IN JANUARY?
JOHN HANCOCK

American statesman and a leader of the American Revolution
He was the first person to sign the Declaration of Independence.
BORN   January 12, 1737, in Quincy, Massachusetts

SATURDAY
January 10

Record cold in Europe; temperatures are 20 to 50 degrees below normal. It's so cold in Sweden that people are advised not to wash!

SUNDAY
January 11

In the U.S., it's too warm! For the first time in 101 years, 1,000 tons of machine-made snow have to be brought by volunteers to the Winter Carnival grounds in St. Paul, Minnesota.

MONDAY
January 12

In London, England, Big Ben's chimes freeze.

TUESDAY
January 13

From studying a single gene, scientists succeed in tracing humans back to a common ancestor in Africa who lived 200,000 years ago.

WEDNESDAY
January 14

Michael Jackson films a Pepsi commercial with Bubbles the roller-skating chimp in Culver City, California.

THURSDAY
January 15

Full Moon

The U.S. Navy launches a Trident II intercontinental ballistic missile from Cape Canaveral, Florida, in its first land-based test.

FRIDAY
January 16

The president of Ecuador, León Febres Cordero, is kidnapped by Ecuadoran air force commandos!

SATURDAY
January 17

In New York City, 16 snakes stolen from the Bronx Zoo are recovered after an anonymous tip leads police to an apartment where the snakes are being kept.

SUNDAY
January 18

National Pizza Week • Donn Nauert of Austin, Texas, is named Video Game Player of the Year at the North American Tournament of Champions in Los Angeles, California.

MONDAY
January 19

Martin Luther King Day • Bells in 50 states are rung at exactly 12:30 P.M. (EST) in honor of the civil rights leader.

TUESDAY
January 20

The first magazine for U.S. grandparents, called *Grandparents,* hits newsstands today, featuring an article "How to Choose Toys for Grandkids."

WEDNESDAY
January 21

Wildlife officials in Seattle, Washington, are trying to catch 6 hungry sea lions that are eating all the spawning trout in the Ballard Locks!

BIRTHDAYS IN 1987

The Alarm Clock 200 Years!

The U.S. Constitution 200 years!

The Golden Gate Bridge 50 Years!

Cracker Jack Prizes 75 Years!

Sherlock Holmes 100 Years!

The Girl Scouts of America 75 Years!

The Appalachian Trail 50 YEARS!

The Trampoline 50 years!

Nylon 50 Years!

Daffy Duck 50 Years!

THURSDAY
January 22

Glenn Tremml breaks the distance record for human-powered flight in his light Eagle aircraft, a cross between a windmill and a bicycle. He goes 37.2 miles before landing at Edwards Air Force Base in California.

FRIDAY
January 23

Soviets have found the antarctic research station that disappeared last fall when part of an ice shelf broke away.

SATURDAY
January 24

10,000 people march in a civil rights demonstration in the all-white town of Cumming, Georgia (population 2,000).

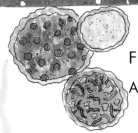

FUN FACT '87

Americans eat 75 acres of pizza a day.

SUNDAY
January 25

A record number of TV viewers (130,000,000) watch the New York Giants beat the Denver Broncos in football's Super Bowl XXI, 39–20.

MONDAY
January 26

The President's Council on Physical Fitness and Sports reports that American children are in "disgraceful" physical condition, even though 9 out of 10 parents believe their kids are in good shape.

TUESDAY
January 27

President Reagan delivers the State of the Union message to Congress. • A huge ticker tape parade welcomes the New York Giants, winners of the Super Bowl, back to New Jersey.

WEDNESDAY
January 28

Because of recent kidnappings, the U.S. State Department bans all travel to Lebanon by U.S. citizens.

THURSDAY
January 29

The largest robot exhibit in the U.S. opens at the Boston Museum of Science, featuring robots that paint pictures and play cards! • In England, swans and ducks turn pink when dye is accidentally spilled into the river Ouse.

FRIDAY
January 30

Surgeons in Buffalo, New York, remove a cataract from the eye of Sandy, a performing harbor seal, to try to save her career at the Niagara Falls Aquarium.

SATURDAY
January 31

Over Cerritos, California, an Aeroméxico jet just misses hitting a single-engine plane.

IRAN ATTACKS IRAQ

FIRST $1 TRILLION BUDGET SUBMITTED TO CONGRESS

COKE IS COMING TO RUSSIA

62-YEAR-OLD WOMAN SAVES FALLING WINDOW WASHER

February

The name February comes from the Latin *Februa,* which means "feast of purification."

SUNDAY
February 1

In Scottsdale, Arizona, a Marc Chagall painting worth $490,000 is discovered missing.

MONDAY
February 2

Groundhog Day • 5 U.S. astronauts begin training for the first shuttle mission since the *Challenger* exploded in January 1986.

TUESDAY
February 3

Canadian scientists report they have found a 73,000,000-year-old Troödon dinosaur fossil which proves that birds descended directly from dinosaurs.

WEDNESDAY
February 4

Dennis Conner, aboard the yacht *Stars and Stripes,* wins the America's Cup back from the Australians, who have had it since they won the race in 1983.

THURSDAY
February 5

2 men are arrested for being part of the largest counterfeiting operation in U.S. history, involving at least $17,700,000 of bogus money!

FRIDAY
February 6

Soviet cosmonauts Yuri Romanenko and Aleksandr Laveikin blast off toward the orbiting space station *Mir.*

SATURDAY
February 7

The 2 Soviet spacemen in their *Soyuz* spacecraft dock with *Mir,* in the first automatic docking with the space station. • In Asahikawa, Japan, an 87-foot-high snow palace is unveiled.

SUNDAY
February 8

FORGETFUL ROBBER: A man in Stockton, California, orders 3 cheeseburgers at a drive-up window, then leaves, saying he forgot his note. He returns minutes later with a gun and a note demanding money!

MONDAY
February 9

Ralph Jones wins the ARCA 200 late-model stock car race in Daytona Beach, Florida, when another driver runs out of gas 2 laps from the end of the race.

WHO ELSE WAS BORN IN FEBRUARY?
JUDY BLUME

U.S. writer
She is the author of many books for children and young adults, including *Are You There, God? It's Me, Margaret* and *Tales of a Fourth Grade Nothing*.
BORN February 12, 1938, in Elizabeth, New Jersey

TUESDAY
February 10
At an auction in London, Richard Wright of Birchrunville, Pennsylvania, pays the world-record price of $8,580 for an 84-year-old teddy bear named Archibald.

WEDNESDAY
February 11
Health experts report that people need 1,000 milligrams of calcium per day to keep their bones strong and healthy.

THURSDAY
February 12
Lincoln's birthday • The U.S. Postal Service issues a 14-cent stamp in honor of Julia Ward Howe, who wrote the words to "The Battle Hymn of the Republic."

FRIDAY
February 13
Full Moon
It's Friday the 13th. • Camel and ostrich races in Riverside County, California!

SATURDAY
February 14
Valentine's Day • 13 tornadoes rip through Oklahoma, Texas, Louisiana, and Mississippi.

SUNDAY
February 15
The Daytona 500 auto race in Daytona Beach, Florida, is won by Bill Elliott, with an average speed of 176.263 miles per hour.

MONDAY
February 16
To celebrate the 93d birthday of Hershey's Cocoa, a 93-layer cake, made with ingredients including 56 pounds of cocoa, 280 pounds of sugar, and 790 eggs, is featured at the Great American Chocolate Festival in Hershey, Pennsylvania.

FUN FACT '87

A special shoe has been invented that allows a person to walk on water.

COOL!

1987: CHINESE YEAR OF THE HARE

January 29, 1987–February 16, 1988

According to legend, Buddha summoned all the animals in the world to him one New Year, promising them a reward. Only 12 obeyed, and he gave them each a year; the Rat arrived first, so he got the first year! The order of the 12-year cycle is Rat, Ox, Tiger, Hare, Dragon, Snake, Horse, Sheep, Monkey, Rooster, Dog, and Pig.

Hares are usually quiet and kind, but they can be moody. They get along well with Sheep and Dogs but not with Roosters, Tigers, or Horses.

Famous Hares: Albert Einstein, Joseph Stalin, Sally Ride, Marie Curie, Booker T. Washington, Sting, Dave Winfield, and Whitney Houston.

Albert Einstein   Marie Curie   Sting

TUESDAY
February 17

A California man parachutes out of a small plane into a landfill near the World Trade Center in New York City. He is arrested for reckless endangerment.

WEDNESDAY
February 18

Last day of the American International Toy Fair in New York City. On exhibit are Cabbage Patch Talking Kids. Any Cabbage Patch Talking Kid that gets within 20 feet of another begins to talk!

THURSDAY
February 19

A team of ocean scientists reports finding a strange new world inside an underwater volcano near Hawaii—complete with 2-foot-long fish with huge mouths, sharp fangs, blue eyes, and front legs.

FRIDAY
February 20

Cosmonauts Yuri Romanenko and Aleksandr Laveikin are performing their first scientific experiments on board the space station *Mir*.

SATURDAY
February 21

Health experts in Washington, D.C., discover that antibodies in animal feed may be causing salmonellosis (a type of food poisoning) in humans.

SUNDAY
February 22

Washington's birthday • Rainbow lovers flock to see the 80-foot indoor rainbow and soap-bubble rainbows on display at the New York Hall of Science in New York City.

MONDAY
February 23

SAFE AND SOUND: Rescuers in Woodbury, Tennesseé, find 4 missing cave explorers trapped in an air pocket in a flooded cave.

TUESDAY
February 24

Ian Shelton, an astronomer working in Chile, spots a supernova (exploding star) that has the brilliance of a billion suns. It's the closest supernova spotted since 1604—163,000 light-years away from earth.

WEDNESDAY
February 25

South Carolina and Georgia hold tornado drills as part of Tornado Awareness Week in the U.S.

THURSDAY
February 26

In Orlando, Florida, Terry Parlier paddles into the underground storm-drainage system in a small boat to try to trap an 8-foot-long alligator that has been chasing sewer workers!

FRIDAY
February 27

Basketball star Cheryl Miller and TV actresses Justine Bateman and Tina Yothers receive the first Girl Hero awards from the Girls Club of America.

SATURDAY
February 28

Soviet leader Mikhail Gorbachev says he would agree to the elimination of all medium-range nuclear missiles in Europe.

HEAD OF WORLD'S LARGEST DRUG RING CAPTURED

COYOTE CHEWS SEATS OFF 14 SNOWMOBILES

LONGEST U.S. STEEL-INDUSTRY STRIKE IN HISTORY ENDS

KILLER AVALANCHE IN BRECKENRIDGE, COLORADO

March

*M*arch is named for the Roman god of war, Mars.

BIRTHSTONE *Aquamarine*

SUNDAY
March 1

Chicago, Illinois, begins a yearlong 150th birthday celebration with a Grand Wabano Dance. • Bully, the Mississippi State bulldog, wins the National College Mascot Championship in Orlando, Florida.

MONDAY
March 2

11-year-old Benjamin Barreaux of Millburn, New Jersey, wins $500 from his mother for not watching any TV for a whole year!

TUESDAY
March 3

15 pancake flippers in Liberal, Kansas, compete with those in Olney, England, in the International Pancake Day Race. Olney's Elizabeth Bartlett wins for the 2d year in a row, completing the 415-yard course and 2 flips in 64.7 seconds.

WEDNESDAY
March 4

FALSE ALARM: The National Weather Service accidentally sends a tornado warning to Barber County, Kansas!

THURSDAY
March 5

A rare Baringo giraffe is born at the Bronx Zoo in New York City and is named James IV.

FRIDAY
March 6

A small rocket carrying an experiment for the University of California at Berkeley explodes just 20 seconds after lifting off from Poker Flats, Alaska.

SATURDAY
March 7

The biggest street festival in the U.S.—the 10th annual Carnival Miami—takes place in Miami, Florida. It's 23 blocks long!

SUNDAY
March 8

Shinji Kazama of Tokyo, Japan, leaves Ward Hunt Island in Canada to ride to the North Pole on a motorcycle.

MONDAY
March 9

Geologists have found rock samples from 2 miles deep in the earth that suggest that Florida was once part of Africa.

WHO ELSE WAS BORN IN MARCH?
ALBERT EINSTEIN

U.S./Swiss/German physicist
He is most famous for his theory of relativity,
which became a basis for the development of
nuclear energy.
BORN March 14, 1879, in Ulm, Germany

TUESDAY
March 10

A plane carrying 1,800 pounds of gold bricks lands on its belly at Kennedy Airport in New York after its landing gear malfunctions.

WEDNESDAY
March 11

University of Chicago scientists report that there is diamond dust—microscopic diamonds older than the Sun and the Earth—floating in space.

THURSDAY
March 12

The Girl Scouts of America celebrates its 75th birthday. 2,000 Girl Scouts take part in a special ceremony in Washington, D.C., with first lady Nancy Reagan, and the U.S. Postal Service issues a 22-cent commemorative stamp.

FRIDAY
March 13

WORLD'S FIRST TOAD TUNNEL: A 6-inch-wide, 40-foot-long tunnel for toads opens in England; now they can cross under the busy highway to the breeding ponds on the other side and not get squashed!

SATURDAY
March 14

U.S. Coast Guard helicopters rescue 37 people (including a baby) from a sinking Soviet freighter caught in a bad storm off New Jersey's coast.

SUNDAY
March 15

Full Moon

It's Buzzard Day in Hinckley, Ohio! The town's buzzards return for the summer every year on this day. The first buzzard is spotted at 9:17 A.M.

MONDAY
March 16

The 37 Soviets who were rescued on Saturday go sightseeing and shopping for new clothes in Washington, D.C., before their flight home tomorrow.

TUESDAY
March 17

St. Patrick's Day • A violent tornado whips through Texas.

WEDNESDAY
March 18

For the 2d year in a row, Susan Butcher wins the Iditarod Trail Sled-Dog Race, covering the 1,100 miles from Anchorage to Nome in 11 days, 2 hours, 5 minutes, 13 seconds.

THURSDAY
March 19

Swallow Day in San Juan Capistrano, California. More than 3,000 people turn out to greet the swallows returning from Argentina, where they spend the winter.

FRIDAY
March 20

Scientists have found 15,000,000-year-old fossils of whales 5,000 feet up in the Andes, proving the mountains were once under the sea.

SATURDAY
March 21

Spring equinox • The California Strawberry Advisory Board sends strawberries to TV weather forecasters in 21 cities throughout the state, who eat them on TV!

SUNDAY
March 22

The annual Weird Beard Contest is held in Miami, Florida. No animal hair or fish scales allowed.

MONDAY
March 23

Spring snowstorm hits the Great Plains. • 400 buffalo have been herded by about 50 cowboys back to their summer home in Hooper, Colorado.

TUESDAY
March 24

The prime minister of France signs a $2 billion contract to build the first Disneyland in Europe. It will be located 20 miles east of Paris.

WEDNESDAY
March 25

Archaeologists in Honduras report a fabulous new discovery of artifacts—including beautiful jade carvings and a shell that may contain the blood of an ancient Mayan king.

THURSDAY
March 26

NASA is forced to blow up an Atlas-Centaur rocket 51 seconds after liftoff. It was off course.

FUN FACT '87

In 1896, Albert Einstein got a D on his high school report card.

SOME INVENTIONS OF 1987

Fortune-cookie folding machine
Velcro convertible pants
Water-walking shoes
Antismoker hat
Lunch-box alarm
Geep (a cross between a goat and a sheep)

Edible pet-food spoon
Refrigerated pet-food bowl
Bubble Thing
Dual camera
Shoelace magnets
Swivel headrest

FRIDAY
March 27

In special races in Memphis, Tennessee, robots ride ponies!

SATURDAY
March 28

Prime Minister Margaret Thatcher arrives in the Soviet Union. She's the first British prime minister to visit in 12 years.

SUNDAY
March 29

There is an annular solar eclipse, when the sun appears to make a ring around the Moon, visible in South America, the South Atlantic, Africa, and the Indian Ocean.

MONDAY
March 30

Indiana wins the NCAA basketball championship, 74–73, defeating Syracuse. • A painting by Vincent van Gogh, *Sunflowers,* is sold in London, England, for the record price of $39,900,000. The anonymous buyer bid over the telephone.

TUESDAY
March 31

A plane runs into a fish in the air over Alaska, near Juneau. The fish was dropped by an eagle. • It's so cold in Texas that peaches are frozen on the trees!

18 MOBSTERS CONVICTED IN NEW YORK

2 EARTHQUAKES DEVASTATE JUNGLE IN ECUADOR

THOUSANDS OF HONEYBEES DIE IN FLORIDA

4-YEAR-OLDS PICKET CITY HALL IN MILWAUKEE, WI

April

*T*he name April comes from the Latin *aperire,* which means "to open." April is known as the time of budding.

BIRTHSTONE *Diamond*

WEDNESDAY
April 1

April Fools' Day • After 4 years, Steven Newman of Bethel, Ohio, returns home from walking around the world through 20 countries. He's the first person to walk the 22,500 miles alone.

THURSDAY
April 2

Heavy rain in Maine is causing rivers to overflow and towns to flood.

FRIDAY
April 3

WORLD'S LARGEST GEM SALE: The late Duchess of Windsor's fabulous jewelry collection is auctioned in Switzerland for $56,281,887.

SATURDAY
April 4

Bubble Thing, a new device that can make soap bubbles 8 feet in diameter, has been patented by New York architect David R. Stein.

SUNDAY
April 5

In Norton, Kansas, Orville and Nellie Obendorf are rescued from their car, where they were trapped for 13 days by snowdrifts; they survived by eating Girl Scout Cookies!

MONDAY
April 6

Will Lindsey of Wallasey, England, sets off from Jiayuguan in central Asia to run along the 1,500-mile Great Wall of China, the longest wall in the world.

FUN FACT '87

There are 5,000,000 more cats than dogs in households in the U.S.

WHO ELSE WAS BORN IN APRIL?
BOOKER T. WASHINGTON

U.S. educator, social reformer
A principal spokesperson for black people, he
established the famous Tuskegee Institute in 1881.
BORN   April 5, 1856, in Franklin County, Virginia

TUESDAY
April 7
Frenchman Bruno Peyron sets out alone from New York
Harbor in his catamaran to try to break the transatlantic solo
sailing record.

WEDNESDAY
April 8
BETTER LATE THAN NEVER: The president of Paraguay finally
gets around to lifting a state of emergency that has been in
effect since 1954!

THURSDAY
April 9
320 years ago, the world's first art exhibition
was held at the Palais-Royale in Paris, France.

FRIDAY
April 10
In England, the world's largest Easter egg is constructed
out of milk chocolate. It is 18 feet, 11½ inches tall.

SATURDAY
April 11
Soviet cosmonauts Yuri Romanenko and Aleksandr Laveikin
go for a space walk that lasts 3½ hours.

SUNDAY
April 12
During a baseball game between the Mets and the Atlanta
Braves at Shea Stadium in New York, a fly ball hits a flying
dove. The ball falls onto the field and turning what should
have been an easy out into a double!

MONDAY
April 13
The world's first underwater hotel has opened in Key Largo,
Florida. Guests must "enter" by going 20 feet below the
water's surface.

TUESDAY
April 14
Full Moon
First day of Passover • On April 14, 1828, Noah
Webster published his first American dictionary.

WEDNESDAY
April 15
Scientists at Stanford University in California unveil a new
device that can split atoms, the Stanford Linear Collider.

1987 AWARDS BOARD

Nobel Peace Prize: Oscar Arias Sanchez
National Teacher of the Year: Donna H. Oliver of Burlington, North Carolina
National Spelling Bee Champion: Stephanie Petit
Female Athlete of the Year: Jackie Joyner-Kersee, track and field
Male Athlete of the Year: Ben Johnson, track and field
Horse of the Year: Ferdinand
Best Movie (Academy Award): *The Last Emperor*
Best Special/Visual Effects (Academy Award): *Innerspace*
Grammy Award (album): U2, *The Joshua Tree*
Grammy Award (single): Paul Simon, "Graceland"
Best children's book (Newbery Medal): *The Whipping Boy*, by Sid Fleischman
Best children's book illustration (Caldecott Medal): *Hey, Al*, by Arthur Yorinks, illustrated by Richard Egielski

THURSDAY
April 16

The U.S. government announces that inventors will now be allowed to patent new forms of animal life they may create through gene splicing or genetic engineering.

FRIDAY
April 17

A great white shark—23 feet, 5 inches long—is caught by Alfred Cutajar off the coast of Malta.

SATURDAY
April 18

In Coolidge, Arizona, sky diver Gregory Robertson free-falls at 200 miles per hour to save fellow parachutist Debbie Williams, who was knocked unconscious during her jump. He pulls her rip cord just 10 seconds before impact!

SUNDAY
April 19

Easter • In Kern County, California, biologists capture the last known wild condor and add it to the 26 other condors at the San Diego Zoo. It is 7 years old and is named AC-9.

MONDAY
April 20

Shinji Kazama reaches the North Pole—on motorcycle. He left from northern Canada on March 8. • The Boston Marathon is won by Toshihiko Seko of Japan (time: 2 hours, 11 minutes, 50 seconds) and by Rosa Mota of Portugal (time: 2 hours, 25 minutes, 21 seconds).

TUESDAY
April 21

Oreo, a dog owned by 11-year-old Jason Rambler, is rescued from where he had fallen 75 feet into a 200-foot-deep gorge in Castille, New York. He had been stranded on a ledge for 27 hours!

Be right there, Oreo!

WEDNESDAY
April 22

Earth Day. It's also Arbor Day, Discovery of Brazil Day, Oklahoma Day, Queen Isabella Day, and Lenin Memorial Day!

THURSDAY
April 23

In Bridgeport, Connecticut, a $17,000,000 building under construction collapses; 8 floors of concrete crash to the ground.

FRIDAY
April 24

In the first test of its kind in the world, scientists spray strawberry fields with bacteria that have had an ice-forming gene deleted. They are hoping to create berries that won't freeze in cold weather.

SATURDAY
April 25

Peter Weber wins his 10th Professional Bowlers Association title and collects $50,000 in Akron, Ohio.

SUNDAY
April 26

Biologists are finding 3-pound poisonous toads in central Florida. They're up to 12 inches long, and they're multiplying quickly!

MONDAY
April 27

TOWN OF ISLIP, N.Y.

The town of Islip, New York, outlaws skateboarding on downtown sidewalks.

TUESDAY
April 28

A rare purple-red diamond weighing less than a carat is sold in New York City for a new world record price of $880,000.

WEDNESDAY
April 29

So far, about 3,000 toads have used the toad tunnel that opened on March 13 in England.

THURSDAY
April 30

Sharon Swanson lands a 24-pound fish called a Pacific crevalle jack in Baja California, Mexico. It's the biggest one ever caught!

GIANT PANDAS ARRIVE AT THE BRONX ZOO FROM CHINA

HOMELESS MAN REUNITED WITH HIS 87-YEAR-OLD MOTHER

LARGEST BONFIRE IN HISTORY IN THE NETHERLANDS

May

*M*ay comes from Maia, who was the Roman goddess of growth, increase, and blossoming.

BIRTHSTONE *Emerald*

FRIDAY
May 1

May Day • The Empire State Building officially opened in New York City on this day in 1931.

SATURDAY
May 2

A horse named Alysheba wins the 113th Kentucky Derby. • In Florida, Walt Disney World greets its 242,831,300th visitor, a number officials say is the number of people who live in the U.S. as of today.

SUNDAY
May 3

In Lawrence Township, New Jersey, a playground opens at Benjamin Franklin Elementary School that has a haunted castle, a dragon slide, and even a hot-air balloon!

MONDAY
May 4

2 Frenchmen become the first people to land at the North Pole in an ultra-light aircraft.

TUESDAY
May 5

Mario Andretti sets a record for the quickest lap in the history of the Indianapolis Motor Speedway by driving his Lola around the track at 218.204 miles per hour.

WEDNESDAY
May 6

The Ringling Brothers Barnum & Bailey Clown College travels to Boise, Idaho, where it will hold auditions for would-be clowns.

THURSDAY
May 7

Philippe Jeantot sails into Newport Harbor in Rhode Island, completing his 27,000-mile solo trip around the world in 134 days, 5 hours, 23 minutes, 56 seconds—a new record!

FRIDAY
May 8

A barge from Long Island (the *Mobro*) carrying 3,100 tons of garbage has been wandering up and down the East Coast and in the Caribbean for 8 weeks, searching for a place to dump its cargo. No one wants it!

WHO ELSE WAS BORN IN MAY?
JOHN F. KENNEDY

U.S. president, 1961–63
The youngest man to be elected president, he was
also the 4th president to be assassinated.
BORN   May 29, 1917, in Brookline, Massachusetts

SATURDAY
May 9

A supercomputer called the Numerical
Aerodynamic Simulation Facility, which
can do 1.72 billion computations a second,
starts operations today.

SUNDAY
May 10

Mother's Day • More than 22,000 run in the London
Marathon in England; the winners are Hiromi Taniguchi of
Japan and Ingrid Kristiansen of Norway.

MONDAY
May 11

Sea lampreys, the bloodsucking "vampires of the deep," are
making a comeback in the Great Lakes; officials are worried
about the safety of the salmon and trout.

TUESDAY
May 12

In New York City, a sculpture by Alberto Giacometti sells for
$3,630,000, the highest price ever paid for a sculpture in an
auction.

WEDNESDAY
May 13

Full Moon

President Marco Vinicio Cerezo Arevalo of Guatemala visits
the U.S. for the first time.

THURSDAY
May 14

On this day in 1973, *Skylab*, the first U.S. space laboratory,
was launched. • The Millstone 3 nuclear power plant in
Waterford, Connecticut, accidentally shuts down.

FRIDAY
May 15

The USSR launches a giant, 197-foot-tall rocket called *Energia*.
It weighs 2,646 tons, has a thrust of more than 4,410 tons,
and is capable of putting a 100-ton space shuttle into orbit!

SATURDAY
May 16

Alysheba, the horse that won the Kentucky Derby on May 2,
wins the Preakness in Baltimore, Maryland.

SUNDAY
May 17

A frog named Sugar Town Dandy leaps 19 feet, 7¼ inches, to win the Calaveras County Jumping Frog Jubilee in California.

MONDAY
May 18

Magic Johnson of the Los Angeles Lakers wins the National Basketball Association's Most Valuable Player Award.

TUESDAY
May 19

The U.S. Senate votes to make William Webster the new head of the CIA.

WEDNESDAY
May 20

A SPA FOR SPOT: A health club for dogs has just opened in Paris, France!

THURSDAY
May 21

An unmanned cargo craft docks with the orbiting Soviet space station *Mir* and delivers food, water, fuel, and equipment to the 2 cosmonauts, who have been in space since February 6.

FRIDAY
May 22

A tornado devastates the town of Saragosa, Texas. Every building in town is flattened.

SATURDAY
May 23

The Soviet Union announces that it is giving up commercial whaling (killing whales for profit).

Thanks!

FUN FACT '87

In 1987, 3 billion baseball cards are printed.

SUNDAY
May 24

47-year-old Al Unser, Sr., becomes the oldest driver to win the Indianapolis 500. It's the 4th time he has won the famous automobile race!

MONDAY
May 25

Memorial Day • In West Covina, California, doctors reattach a 7-year-old's ear after it is retrieved from the stomach of a Doberman pinscher that had bitten it off.

TUESDAY
May 26

Scientists successfully transplant a human gene into a monkey's bone marrow cells.

WEDNESDAY
May 27

In Brigham City, Utah, a new space shuttle booster rocket passes its first test.

GOLDEN GATE BRIDGE PARTY

250,000 people crowd the Golden Gate Bridge in San Francisco, California, for the bridge's 50th anniversary celebration—causing the arched bridge to flatten out from so much weight! 500,000 people have to be turned away, because the bridge is already so crowded, authorities are afraid it may fall down. The all-day, $3,000,000 celebration includes fireworks and the lighting of the bridge's 746-foot-high towers.

THURSDAY
May 28

UNEXPECTED GUEST: 19-year-old Matthias Rust of West Germany lands his small, single-engine plane in the middle of Moscow's Red Square. No one knows how he managed to get through the Soviet military defense system!

FRIDAY
May 29

The bust of Thomas Jefferson that was the model for his portrait on the U.S. nickel is sold for a record $2,860,000 in New York City.

SATURDAY
May 30

For the first time in 7 years, the Soviet Union has ended the blocking of radio broadcasting into the country.

SUNDAY
May 31

The Edmonton Oilers beat the Philadelphia Flyers to win hockey's Stanley Cup.

IRAQI PLANE BOMBS U.S. SHIP IN PERSIAN GULF

STEPHANIE PETIT WINS NATIONAL SPELLING BEE

MANUSCRIPT OF 9 MOZART SYMPHONIES SOLD FOR A RECORD $4,340,000

THREE-WAY HEART TRANSPLANT IN BALTIMORE, MD.

June

June is named for the Latin *juniores,* meaning "youths," or from the goddess Juno.

BIRTHSTONE *Pearl*

MONDAY
June 1

At the London Zoo in England, a baby gorilla named Kamili (Swahili for "perfect") is born.

TUESDAY
June 2

New evidence, including stone tools, shows that humans reached Australia 5,000 years earlier than was previously thought.

WEDNESDAY
June 3

SOMETHING'S FISHY: About 10,000 pounds of fish have been stolen this season from fishing vessels in Massachusetts.

THURSDAY
June 4

In Madrid, Spain, Danny Harris beats Edwin Moses in the 400-meter hurdles, ending the track star's record 10-year, 122-race winning streak.

FRIDAY
June 5

Comic book superhero Spider-Man marries longtime girlfriend Mary Jane Watson in a mock wedding held just before a baseball game begins at Shea Stadium in New York.

SATURDAY
June 6

A horse named Bet Twice wins the Belmont Stakes—by an amazing 14 lengths.

FUN FACT '87

Hey, how about that!

Sharks' teeth fall out when they bite something; the teeth grow back later!

WHO ELSE WAS BORN IN JUNE?
ANNE FRANK

German-Jewish writer and Holocaust victim
Her diary about hiding from the Nazis for 2 years
during World War II became famous after her
death.
BORN June 12, 1929, in Frankfurt am Main,
Germany

SUNDAY
June 7

In Alaska, a mountain climber tumbles 1,500 feet down Mount McKinley, stopping just before falling into an enormous crevasse. He is only bruised!

MONDAY
June 8

RUSSIAN BUGS: Soviet listening devices are found in the chancery building of the new U.S. Embassy in Moscow.

TUESDAY
June 9

Lightning accidentally sets off 3 small rockets that were poised on a launching pad at Wallops Island, Virginia, and sends them zooming out to sea.

WEDNESDAY
June 10

Telephone company officials say that their new fiber-optic cables, which are being strung along the ocean floor, are being damaged by shark bites.

THURSDAY
June 11

Full Moon

Margaret Thatcher wins a 3d term as prime minister of Great Britain.

FRIDAY
June 12

The 2 cosmonauts aboard Soviet space station *Mir* make their 2d walk in space, attaching a panel to the surface of *Mir* that will be used for solar batteries.

SATURDAY
June 13

Harvard wins the National Intercollegiate Men's Rowing Championship in a record time of 5 minutes, 35.17 seconds, beating Brown by only 46 hundredths of a second!

SUNDAY
June 14

The Los Angeles Lakers win the NBA Basketball Championship, defeating the Boston Celtics 106–93.

| MONDAY June 15 | On this day in 1902, Justin Clark, playing with a baseball team in Corsicana, Texas, hit 8 home runs in one game. No professional baseball player has ever topped that record. |

| TUESDAY June 16 | Tom McClean sets out from Newfoundland, Canada, to row across the Atlantic Ocean for the 2d time. He's already sailed across it twice! |

| WEDNESDAY June 17 | BIKE AID '87: About 160 bicycle riders leave from 5 western cities to ride across the country to raise money for the poor and hungry. |

| THURSDAY June 18 | Geologists report the discovery of a 28-mile-wide, 1.7-mile-deep undersea crater, 125 miles east of Nova Scotia, Canada. They think it was formed by the impact of a comet. |

| FRIDAY June 19 | Canadian astronomers say they have found evidence of the existence of large planets outside the Solar System—orbiting as many as 7 stars! |

| SATURDAY June 20 | In Florida, Tom Gloy wins the 2-hour Grand Prix of Palm Beach in a Ford Mustang. |

| SUNDAY June 21 | Summer solstice • Father's Day • A tornado strikes a mobile-home park near Detroit, Michigan. |

TOP 10 BABY NAMES FOR 1987*

	BOYS	GIRLS
1	Matthew	Jessica
2	Jonathan	Jennifer
3	Brian	Amanda
4	Michael	Sarah
5	Jason	Ashley
6	Daniel	Melissa
7	Christopher	Nicole
8	Joseph	Lauren
9	Andrew	Megan
10	Ryan	Lindsay

*Source: Gerber Products Company.

MONDAY *June 22*	In England, the first day of the Wimbledon lawn tennis championships is postponed because of heavy rain.
TUESDAY *June 23*	Ling-Ling, the giant panda at the National Zoo in Washington, D.C., has a baby.
WEDNESDAY *June 24*	In Alberta, Canada, Kevin Aulenback discovers fossilized dinosaur eggs that contain unhatched dinosaurs. They are 145,000,000 years old, the oldest ever discovered.

THURSDAY *June 25*	The world's largest cherry pie is made in Traverse City, Michigan. It is 17 feet, 6 inches, in diameter, 26 inches deep and weighs more than 28,355 pounds!
FRIDAY *June 26*	A half-bottle of wine, Château Margaux 1784, engraved with the initials of Thomas Jefferson, is sold for a record price of 180,000 francs in Bordeaux, France.
SATURDAY *June 27*	Managua, Nicaragua, holds its first-ever potato festival! • Beatles memorabilia is auctioned off at Sotheby's in New York City for $319,000.
SUNDAY *June 28*	Using X rays and a CAT scan, scientists in Boston examine a 4,500-year-old mummy named Tabes. The results show she had buck teeth and a big nose!
MONDAY *June 29*	3 pilot whales called Notch, Tag, and Baby are set free by aquarium workers in the Atlantic Ocean at the Georges Bank, east of Massachusetts. They beached themselves on Cape Cod last December.
TUESDAY *June 30*	All 90 U.S. CH-53-E Super Stallion military helicopters are grounded because of gearbox problems.

TOM SCHULER WINS CORE STATES BICYCLE CHAMPION-SHIP

SNOW WHITE GETS A STAR ON THE HOLLYWOOD WALK OF FAME

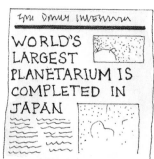

WORLD'S LARGEST PLANETARIUM IS COMPLETED IN JAPAN

July

*T*his month was named to honor Julius Caesar.

BIRTHSTONE *Ruby*

WEDNESDAY
July 1

12-year-old Laine Snyder of Hollywood, Florida, wins the Great American Roach-off for his 2.08-inch-long cockroach, the biggest of 2,000 entries.

THURSDAY
July 2

Richard Branson and Per Lindstrand lift off from Sugarloaf Mountain, Maine, in a huge black and silver hot-air balloon, to travel 3,400 miles across the Atlantic Ocean, a journey no one has ever completed.

FRIDAY
July 3

Branson and Lindstrand jump from their disabled balloon into the sea just as they are within sight of their landing target on the coast of Scotland. The 22-story-high balloon had hit the ground while they were crossing Northern Ireland.

SATURDAY
July 4

 Independence Day • Martina Navratilova beats Steffi Graf to win the women's singles Wimbledon tennis championship in England for the 6th year in a row.

SUNDAY
July 5

Pat Cash wins the men's singles at the Wimbledon tennis tournament. • At Leeds University in England, a competition is being held to build a bridge out of spaghetti that will be strong enough for a car! No macaroni or lasagna allowed.

MONDAY
July 6

In Kennebunk, Maine, an antique fishing lure, which cost less than 50 cents when it was new in 1859, has been sold for the record price of $9,240.

TUESDAY
July 7

Divers are lowered through shark-infested waters off Nantucket, Massachusetts, to search for treasure aboard a sunken ship, the RMS *Republic,* which is believed to contain $1.6 billion in gold coins.

WHO ELSE WAS BORN IN JULY?
OSCAR DE LA RENTA

U.S. fashion designer
He is famous for creating elegant ball gowns for celebrity clients.
BORN July 22, 1932, in Santo Domingo, Dominican Republic

WEDNESDAY
July 8

Rita Norr of New York wins the international Scrabble tournament in Las Vegas, Nevada.

THURSDAY
July 9

In Boston, Massachusetts, a 30-pound lobster named Ralph falls to its death while being weighed at the New England Aquarium.

FRIDAY
July 10

New York City finally agrees to burn the 3,100 tons of Long Island garbage from the floating *Mobro* garbage barge, which has been looking for a resting place for 112 days!

FUN FACT '87

The best-selling cookie in the U.S. is the Oreo.

SATURDAY
July 11
Full Moon

Today the world population hits 5 billion. • In Green Bay, Wisconsin, a circus tent collapses during a performance. Rescuers cut holes in the tent to pull people out.

SUNDAY
July 12

An unarmed Minuteman-3 missile is blown up after its launch from Vandenberg Air Force Base in California, due to flight problems.

MONDAY
July 13

Archaeologists in China have found 1,700 terra-cotta warriors and horses buried in an imperial tomb that they believe to be 1,500 years old.

TUESDAY
July 14

Maurizio Montalbini is brought up to the surface after spending 211 days alone in a cave in Frassasi, Italy. It's a new world record!

WEDNESDAY
July 15

78,000 onions roll off a truck onto a viaduct in the Netherlands; special vacuum vehicles suck them up.

THURSDAY
July 16

The Jim Smith Society's annual Fun Festival is held in Wilmington, North Carolina. More than 50 people named Jim Smith attend. There are 1,400 members of the group in the U.S.

FRIDAY
July 17

Snow White and the Seven Dwarfs, first shown in 1937, is rereleased in 4,000 movie theaters throughout the world.

SATURDAY
July 18

Throughout the U.S., the annual butterfly count is being conducted by the Xerces Society.

WHAT'S HOT IN 1987

Swatch watches	Talking dolls
Ninja Shoes	TV-interactive toys
Disposable cameras	Real Ghostbusters toys
Walkmuffs	Michael's Pets
Snowboarding	Zebugs
Llamas	Gummy Nerds

SUNDAY
July 19

Garlic Week begins. • Flooding in northern Italy. • A koala bear named Blinky Bill returns to the San Diego Zoo after visiting the Buffalo Zoo for a month.

MONDAY
July 20

Near Canyonville, Oregon, 700 fire fighters battle the area's worst forest fire—so far, 10,300 acres have burned!

TUESDAY
July 21

Daniel Hodes of California walks across the Strait of Gibraltar from Africa to Europe in 7 hours, wearing huge plastic pontoons on each foot.

WEDNESDAY
July 22

A space capsule carrying 2 Soviet cosmonauts and Syria's first space traveler blasts off from central Asia. • 10-year-old Christopher Lee Marshall becomes the youngest pilot to fly across the U.S.

THURSDAY
July 23

Yogi the bear has escaped from the Gatorland Zoo in Kissimmee, Florida!

FRIDAY
July 24

91-year-old Hulda Crooks of Loma Linda, California, becomes the oldest woman to climb the 12,389-foot-high Mount Fuji, Japan's highest mountain.

SATURDAY
July 25

The Soviet Union launches a huge space platform, *Cosmos 1870*, into orbit. • In a minisubmarine called *Nautile* and with a robot craft named *Robin*, a French crew dives 2½ miles underwater to the wreck of the *Titanic*, searching for the lost bow of the ship.

SUNDAY
July 26

Stephen Roche of Ireland arrives in Paris, France, winning the 26-day Tour de France bicycle race. • French explorers bring back the first objects from the *Titanic* today: dishes.

MONDAY
July 27

David Kiner arrives in Battery Park, New York, having walked along the Hudson River on water for 57 hours. He is wearing 11-foot-long waterskiing shoes called Skijaks.

TUESDAY
July 28

In New Jersey, Laura Davies becomes the first British golfer to win the U.S. Women's Open.

WEDNESDAY
July 29

A Soviet spacecraft returns to earth with Syria's first astronaut and 2 Soviet cosmonauts, after a visit to orbiting space station *Mir*. Aleksandr Laveikin, one of the cosmonauts, had to be replaced because of heart problems.

THURSDAY
July 30

A 19-foot great white shark sinks a 20-foot boat, spilling 2 fishermen and a 12-year-old boy into the ocean near Hawaii. They swim 9 miles to shore with a pack of sharks following them!

FRIDAY
July 31

A tornado whips through Edmonton in western Canada, tossing cars on a freeway into the air.

MASSIVE OIL SPILL IN ALASKA'S COOK INLET

1,000,000 GOLD AND 10,000,000 SILVER CONSTITUTION COINS MINTED

MONKEY GETS LOOSE ON CARGO PLANE

August

*A*ugust was named in honor of Roman emperor Augustus, whose lucky month it was.

BIRTHSTONE *Peridot*

SATURDAY
August 1

The U.S. National Hot-Air Balloon Championships take place in Indianola, Iowa. • 5 tornadoes strike Edmonton in Alberta, Canada.

SUNDAY
August 2

After a 3-day climb, 100-year-old Teiichi Igarashi reaches the top of Mount Fuji in Japan.

MONDAY
August 3

In a plum tree in Cerritos, California, experts discover an African pumpkin fly, the first ever found in North America.

TUESDAY
August 4

Jim Dickson, who is blind, leaves Portsmouth, Rhode Island, to cross the Atlantic Ocean solo in his 36-foot boat called *Eye-Opener*. • 2 planes collide over the Mojave Desert; both land safely!

WEDNESDAY
August 5

MUMPS JUMPS: The federal Centers for Disease Control report that there have been 9,500 known cases of mumps in the first half of 1987, more than there were in all of 1986.

THURSDAY
August 6

The famous Soviet pianist Vladimir O. Feltsman emigrates from the Soviet Union. He arrives in Vienna, Austria, today on his way to the U.S.

FRIDAY
August 7

Suspicious baseball officials take X rays of the bat used by player Howard Johnson to hit a home run in New York last night, to make sure it's made only of wood. It is!

FUN FACT '87

The best-selling record in North America is *White Christmas*, sung by Bing Crosby—170,884,207 copies, as of June 30.

WHO ELSE WAS BORN IN AUGUST?
WHITNEY HOUSTON

U.S. singer
She won a 1986 Grammy Award for top female pop vocalist; her best known hit in 1987 is "How Will I Know."
BORN   August 9, 1963, in Newark, New Jersey

SATURDAY
August 8

SHARK ALERT: A 40-ton finback whale has washed ashore in Amagansett, Long Island, and sharks have come to feed on the carcass.

SUNDAY
August 9

Full Moon

250,000 black South African miners go on strike. • In Atlantic City, New Jersey, the Golden Nugget's 7th annual Sand Castle Contest is held.

MONDAY
August 10

At the Pan American Games in Indianapolis, Indiana, Greg Louganis wins the men's 3-meter springboard competition and becomes the first 3-time winner of a diving event at the Pan Am Games.

TUESDAY
August 11

— Hey, check this out!

A mysterious 2,500-year-old dog cemetery has been found by archaeologists in Israel, containing 120 dog graves from about 450 B.C.

WEDNESDAY
August 12

Divers from the French expedition find one of the *Titanic*'s strongboxes and want to bring it to the surface. Other experts object, saying the wreck should be left as is.

THURSDAY
August 13

A small plane almost hits President Reagan's helicopter, coming within 200 feet of it as the helicopter nears the president's ranch in Santa Barbara, California.

FRIDAY
August 14

A blue whale has been spotted off the coast of New England, the 4th one to be seen in the area since October of 1986.

SATURDAY
August 15

Scott Johnson wins an all-around gold medal for gymnastics at the Pan American Games, setting a new Pan Am Games record. • Tornado hits Battle Lake, Minnesota.

SUNDAY
August 16

15-year-old Donna Klett of Stow, Ohio, wins the National Jigsaw Puzzle Championship single's title in Athens, Ohio, for finishing a 500-piece puzzle in 1 hour, 13 minutes, 45 seconds.

MONDAY
August 17

Tom McClean arrives in London, England, after rowing across the Atlantic Ocean and is greeted by a 6-gun salute. He has set a new world record for transatlantic rowing: 54 days, 23 hours.

TUESDAY
August 18

American journalist Charles Glass slips out of his chains, locks up his sleeping guards, and escapes from his Muslim kidnappers in Beirut, Lebanon.

WEDNESDAY
August 19

About 160 cyclists taking part in Bike Aid 87 arrive at the United Nations in New York, having raised more than $200,000 to feed the hungry. They left from 5 western cities on June 17.

THURSDAY
August 20

An airplane pilot passes a group of parachutists—and almost hits one—in the air over Chicago, Illinois. Another pilot reports seeing red balloons!

FRIDAY
August 21

Sergeant Clayton Lonetree is convicted of spying for the Soviet Union. He's the first U.S. marine to be convicted of espionage.

SATURDAY
August 22

French explorers have brought up a suitcase from the sunken wreck of the *Titanic*. The case contains jewels and money.

SUNDAY
August 23

The world's smartest person, Marilyn Mach vos Savant, marries the man who invented the artificial heart, Robert Jarvik, in New York City.

MONDAY
August 24

15 sea otters are caught today off the central coast of California. Federal wildlife agents are moving the otters in order to save the species from extinction that would occur if there was a spill from nearby oil drilling.

TUESDAY
August 25

The World's Largest Yard Sale is being held! It runs for 350 miles through Tennessee and Kentucky.

WEDNESDAY
August 26

NICE CATCH: Winston Baker sets a freshwater fishing record by catching an 8-pound, 12-ounce spotted gar in the Tennessee River in Alabama.

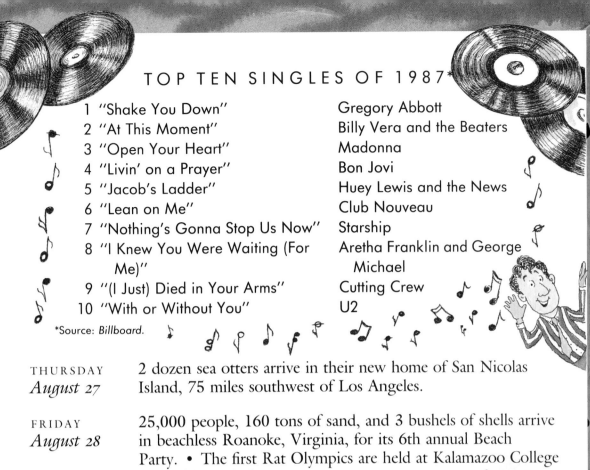

TOP TEN SINGLES OF 1987*

1	"Shake You Down"	Gregory Abbott
2	"At This Moment"	Billy Vera and the Beaters
3	"Open Your Heart"	Madonna
4	"Livin' on a Prayer"	Bon Jovi
5	"Jacob's Ladder"	Huey Lewis and the News
6	"Lean on Me"	Club Nouveau
7	"Nothing's Gonna Stop Us Now"	Starship
8	"I Knew You Were Waiting (For Me)"	Aretha Franklin and George Michael
9	"(I Just) Died in Your Arms"	Cutting Crew
10	"With or Without You"	U2

Source: Billboard.

THURSDAY
August 27

2 dozen sea otters arrive in their new home of San Nicolas Island, 75 miles southwest of Los Angeles.

FRIDAY
August 28

25,000 people, 160 tons of sand, and 3 bushels of shells arrive in beachless Roanoke, Virginia, for its 6th annual Beach Party. • The first Rat Olympics are held at Kalamazoo College in Michigan. A dozen rats compete.

SATURDAY
August 29

In Williamsport, Pennsylvania, the Hua Lian team of Taiwan beats the Irvine squad from California, 21–1, in the Little League World Series.

SUNDAY
August 30

Canadian Ben Johnson breaks the world record for the 100-meter race in Rome, Italy, and becomes the fastest man in the world. Time: 9.83 seconds. • 20 large pizzas from Grotto Pizza in Rehoboth Beach, Delaware, are delivered by boat to Dutch sailors in a freighter 12 miles offshore!

MONDAY
August 31

George Bucsko wins the 10th annual New Jersey Championship Tomato Weigh-in with a 4.352-pound tomato.

U.S. MARINE SPY CLAYTON LONETREE SENTENCED TO 30 YEARS IN PRISON

PRESIDENT ADMITS SOME MISTAKES IN IRAN-CONTRA AFFAIR

SANDPIPER SETS SPEED RECORD FOR BIRDS

LYNNE COX SWIMS FROM THE U.S. TO THE SOVIET UNION

September

*T*he name September comes from the Latin *septem,* meaning "seven." This was the seventh month of the old Roman calendar.

BIRTHSTONE *Sapphire*

TUESDAY
September 1

3,100 tons of garbage from the *Mobro* garbage barge is finally burned in Brooklyn, after being turned away by 6 states and 3 countries. The barge has been looking for a dumping place for 165 days!

WEDNESDAY
September 2

Leaders of 41 French-speaking countries meet in Quebec, Canada, to promote better understanding among their nations.

THURSDAY
September 3

NASA celebrates the 10th anniversary of the launching of the *Voyager 2* spacecraft. It's now about 3.5 billion miles from Earth, on its way to Neptune. It will make its closest approach to the planet in 1989.

FRIDAY
September 4

A state of emergency is declared in northern California as huge forest fires destroy hundreds of thousands of acres.

SATURDAY
September 5

A 22-hour operation begins to separate 7-month-old Siamese twins Patrick and Benjamin Binder, who are connected at the back of their heads. 70 people are involved in the operation.

SUNDAY
September 6

This week is National Rub-a-Bald-Head Week. • The Frisbee Festival is held in White Plains, Maryland.

MONDAY
September 7

Full Moon

Labor Day • Chairman Erich Honecker becomes the first East German leader to visit West Germany.

TUESDAY
September 8

On this day in 1883, the final spike of the Northern Pacific Railroad was driven in at Gold Creek, Montana, after 13 years of construction.

WHO ELSE WAS BORN IN SEPTEMBER?
GRANDMA MOSES (born ANNA MARY ROBERTSON)

U.S. painter
She is best known for her autobiographical paintings of country life.
BORN September 7, 1860, in Greenwich, New York

WEDNESDAY
September 9

In Israel, archaeologists have found a 1,700-year-old mosaic of a beautiful woman who is being called the Mona Lisa of Roman Palestine.

THURSDAY
September 10

Swap Ideas Day • A refrigerated pet bowl designed to keep pet food fresh has been patented by William H. Crowell of Lansdale, Pennsylvania.

FRIDAY
September 11

The original Winnie-the-Pooh, now 65 years old, goes on display at the public library in New York City.

SATURDAY
September 12

Vince Coleman, left fielder for the St. Louis Cardinals, becomes the first major league player to steal 100 bases in 3 consecutive seasons.

SUNDAY
September 13

Grandparents' Day • A llama on the loose is chased and lassoed by a police car and ambulance in Dallas, Texas.

MONDAY
September 14

In New York City, a man weighing 1,190 pounds gets stuck in his bedroom doorway and has to be rescued by fire fighters.

TUESDAY
September 15

A European Space Agency rocket carrying 2 communications satellites is launched, marking the reentry of European nations into commercial space projects.

WEDNESDAY
September 16

24 countries sign an international treaty to protect the atmosphere's ozone layer from further destruction by chlorofluorocarbons.

THURSDAY
September 17

200th anniversary of the signing of the U.S. Constitution. • The world's tallest sand castle is built in Santa Monica, California, by Todd Vander Pluym. It is 28-feet-high and has 5,603 windows!

FRIDAY
September 18

President Reagan announces that a pact with the Soviet Union about banning medium-range and short-range missiles will be signed later this year.

SATURDAY
September 19

Happy birthday, Mickey Mouse! He was introduced by Walt Disney in a 1928 cartoon called *Steamboat Willie*.

SUNDAY
September 20

INTERNATIONAL EXCHANGE: The *New York Times* reports that Fred Rogers is going to appear on the Soviet children's TV program *Good Night, Kiddies*, and the host of that show, Tatyana Vedeneyeva, will appear on *Mr. Rogers' Neighborhood*.

MONDAY
September 21

Susan Butcher, 2-time winner of the Iditarod Trail Sled-Dog Race, is named Professional Sportswoman of the Year by the Women's Sports Foundation.

THE OZONE LAYER

Ozone is a poisonous blue gas with a strong odor. It can be made by shooting oxygen with a high-voltage electrical charge. The upper atmosphere of the earth contains a natural layer of ozone which protects the planet from the sun's harmful ultraviolet rays. Since the early 1970s, many scientists have suspected that the ozone layer is being depleted by man-made chemicals used in refrigeration, in some solvents, and in spray cans. These chemicals, called *chlorofluorocarbons*, remain in the atmosphere for a long time and have been found to destroy ozone molecules.

In 1987, scientists find a huge hole in the ozone layer over Antarctica, which alarms people worldwide. On September 16, an international treaty to reduce the production of chlorofluorocarbons is signed in Montreal, Canada, by 24 countries.

"WE THE PEOPLE . . ."

Philadelphia: To celebrate the 200th anniversary of the U.S. Constitution on September 17, a replica of the Liberty Bell is rung, flags are waved, the Mormon Tabernacle Choir sings the national anthem, and there is a 2-mile parade with 30 floats. Independence Hall is filled with balloons, and President Reagan makes a speech.

The U.S. Constitution, which was signed by state delegates in 1787, defines the rights of citizens and of states, as well as the structures and powers of the federal government.

TUESDAY
September 22

The National Football League Players Association goes on strike.

WEDNESDAY
September 23

Autumn equinox • Rick Valenzuela and Melissa Dexter, doing the cha-cha, win the United States Ballroom Dance Championships in Miami, Florida.

WHAT IS THE CHA-CHA?

The cha-cha is a Latin American dance which gets its name from seed pods produced by certain plants in the West Indies. These pods (called *cha-cha*, *tcha-tcha*, or *kwa-kwa*) are used to make a small rattle which is also called a cha-cha. In Haiti, the leader of a voodoo band uses such a rattle to set the time—or keep the rhythm—in dancing and singing. The cha-cha, in which dancers dance to the count of slow, slow, slow, quick quick (or 1,2,3, cha-cha) was introduced to the U.S. in 1954, and by 1959 it had become the country's most popular dance. In 1987, the cha-cha is the winning dance at the U.S. Ballroom Dance Championships!

THURSDAY *September 24*	First day of Rosh Hashanah • For the first time, strange fish called coelacanths have been photographed deep in the Indian Ocean. They are 5-feet-long, have leglike fins, and often do headstands and swim backward or upside down!
FRIDAY *September 25*	The U.S. Postal Service issues a 22-cent stamp to celebrate the anniversary of the birth of U.S. author William Faulkner.

FUN FACT '87

Snakes crossing a road are 3 times more likely to be squashed than turtles.

SATURDAY *September 26*	Happy birthday, Johnny Appleseed. • On this day in 1871, cement was patented by David O. Saylor.
SUNDAY *September 27*	A government report is released revealing that office workers in some corporations are being spied on by their computers.
MONDAY *September 28*	WATCH THE BIRDIE: A B1 bomber crashes in Colorado after hitting some birds. • Huge avalanche of rocks and mud in Colombia.
TUESDAY *September 29*	The Soviets launch a spacecraft that carries 2 monkeys and some rats, insects, amphibians, and fish, part of an experiment on the effects of weightlessness.
WEDNESDAY *September 30*	A 300-year-old wooden doll is sold in London, England, for a record price: 26,400 British pounds.

YANKEE DON MATTINGLY SETS RECORD FOR GRAND-SLAM

THE DAILY NEWS
SENATOR JOSEPH BIDEN ACCUSED OF PLAGIARISM

ANTI CHOLESTEROL DRUG APPROVED

October

*O*ctober was the eighth month of the old Roman calendar; the name is from the Latin *octo,* meaning "eight."

BIRTHSTONE *Opal*

THURSDAY
October 1

A violent earthquake (6.1 on the Richter scale) strikes Los Angeles. • Soviet cosmonaut Yuri Romanenko breaks the record for human endurance in space—it's his 237th day orbiting earth.

FRIDAY
October 2

Archaeologists report that the tomb of Queen Eurydice, grandmother of Alexander the Great, has been found below Mount Olympus in Greece.

SATURDAY
October 3

Yom Kippur • The U.S. and Canada sign a historic trade agreement after 16 months of negotiating!

SUNDAY
October 4

Mexico's ruling party, which has not lost an election since 1929, names its new presidential candidate, Carlos Salinas de Gortari, to be elected in 1988.

MONDAY
October 5

Officials announce that Saudi Arabia has given $5,000,000 to actor Paul Newman to help build a camp in Connecticut for critically ill children.

TUESDAY
October 6

China's first Kentucky Fried Chicken restaurant opens in Beijing. • Hungry coyotes attack 86 flamingos at the Los Angeles Zoo when keepers accidentally leave the coyotes' pen open. 38 are saved by employees who beat away the coyotes.

WEDNESDAY
October 7

Full Moon

SPACED-OUT CHIMP: On board a Soviet research satellite, a monkey named Yerosha ("troublemaker" in Russian) has freed its left arm from a restraining cuff and is pushing buttons at random—endangering the mission. The craft may have to be brought back to earth!

WHO ELSE WAS BORN IN OCTOBER?
EVEL KNIEVEL (born ROBERT CRAIG KNIEVEL)

U.S. stunt motorcyclist
His most famous stunt was the attempted sky-cycle jump of Snake River Canyon in Idaho in 1974.
BORN   October 17, 1938, in Butte, Montana

THURSDAY
October 8

Bears in Montana are getting drunk on hundreds of tons of corn from a train that derailed in 1985. The corn has fermented, and the bears are eating it.

FRIDAY
October 9

Governor Bob Martinez signs a new law making it illegal to carry guns openly in Florida.

SATURDAY
October 10

BEETLEMANIA: On display at Harvard University in Cambridge, Massachusetts, are more than 5,000 beetles!

SUNDAY
October 11

A strange 3-pound metal object falls out of the sky in Lakeport, California. • An underwater volcano explodes in the south central Pacific Ocean. Violent bubbles filled with hot gas and rocks erupt out of the water.

MONDAY
October 12

The Soviet space capsule with the troublemaker monkey on board lands, thousands of miles off course.

TUESDAY
October 13

Researchers from 2 universities say that katydids in Panama have learned how to dance (to attract females for mating)—rather than sing as they usually do—to avoid being eaten by bats.

WEDNESDAY
October 14

Scientists have found the oldest known boomerang in the world—23,000 years old—in a cave in Poland.

THURSDAY *October 15*	The 24-day National Football League players' strike comes to an end. The players could not get the League to give in on their biggest demand: free agency.
FRIDAY *October 16*	An 18-month-old child is rescued from a well shaft in Midland, Texas. • In Vancouver, Canada, a baby only 2½ hours old has a heart transplant.
SATURDAY *October 17*	First lady Nancy Reagan has surgery for breast cancer at Bethesda Naval Hospital in Maryland.
SUNDAY *October 18*	In Norway, Terje Nordtvedt lands a record-breaking 1,708-pound, 9-ounce Greenland shark!

MONDAY
October 19

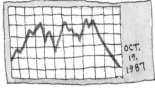

OCT. 19, 1987

BLACK MONDAY: The stock market (the Dow Jones industrial average) falls 508 points, making this the worst day in Wall Street history.

TUESDAY
October 20

Using space-age technology, American experts lower a tiny camera through stone into a pit at the Great Pyramid of Cheops and see a video image of a royal boat buried 4,600 years ago!

FUN FACT '87

A Swiss company has created a watch that is controlled by talking to it!

PLEASE beep me at 5 o'clock.

WEDNESDAY *October 21*	Massachusetts Institute of Technology professor Robert M. Solow is awarded the Nobel Prize in Economics in Stockholm, Sweden.
THURSDAY *October 22*	A rare 1455 copy of the Old Testament of the Gutenberg Bible is sold for $5,390,000 in New York City—the highest price ever paid for a printed book.

$5,390,000

FRIDAY *October 23*	The Research Council in Rome announces that it has remeasured Mount Everest—by satellite. At 29,078 feet, it's definitely the highest mountain in the world.

OCTOBER IS NATIONAL APPLE MONTH

Apples are freshest in October. More than 300 varieties are grown in the U.S. Washington State is the nation's largest apple-growing area. Apples can be red, yellow, or green—or a mixture of colors. How many of these varieties have you eaten?

APPLE	COLOR
Red Delicious	Red
Golden Delicious	Yellow
McIntosh	Red and green
Granny Smith	Green
Cortland	Red and green striped
Idared	Red
Jonathan	Red and Yellow
Mutsu	Yellow/green
Newton Pippin	Green/yellow
Northern Spy	Red and green striped
Winesap	Red

SATURDAY
October 24

51 herds of cattle in England have a new disease called bovine spongiform encephalopathy, otherwise known as—mad cow disease!

SUNDAY
October 25

The Minnesota Twins win their first baseball World Series, defeating the St. Louis Cardinals, 4–2, in the seventh and last game.

MONDAY
October 26

A Titan 34D rocket carrying a secret payload is launched from Vandenberg Air Force Base in California.

THE TEST OF MOUNT EVEREST

The famous Mount Everest, located in the Himalayas on the border between Nepal and Tibet, is the world's highest mountain. In 1852, the Survey Department of the Government of India declared the mountain to be the highest on earth, using special readings called theodolite readings, which were taken in 1849 and 1850. However, in March 1987, that fact was challenged by a U.S. expedition who claimed that K2 (also known as *Chogori*), a mountain in Pakistan, was higher than Everest by about 200 feet. The dispute lasted for months until scientists finally proved, using 4 navigation satellites to take measurements, that Mount Everest was still the highest mountain in the world. On October 23, officials in Rome announce the results:

Mount Everest - 29,078 feet
K2 - 28,238 feet
Mount Everest wins by 840 feet!

TUESDAY
October 27
The first baby ever to be born in an airplane was delivered over Miami, Florida, on this day in 1929.

WEDNESDAY
October 28
At 9:30 A.M., bags of money spill out of an armored truck onto a highway in Columbus, Ohio, sending $1,000,000 in 20-, 50-, and 100-dollar bills floating over the crowded highway.

THURSDAY
October 29
The Anti-Defamation League of B'nai B'rith reports that violent gangs of youths called skinheads are terrorizing major cities in the U.S.

FRIDAY
October 30
Researchers in Davis, California, have crossed goats with sheep and are raising a new kind of animal: geeps!

SATURDAY
October 31
Halloween • Two sky divers accidentally drop a pumpkin from 2,000 feet; it smashes through a roof and lands on the kitchen floor of a house in Hinckley, Illinois.

COUPLE WINS LARGEST LOTTERY IN NORTH AMERICAN HISTORY $46,000,000

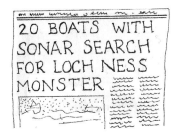

20 BOATS WITH SONAR SEARCH FOR LOCH NESS MONSTER

U.S. STOCK MARKET COLLAPSES

November

Novembet was the ninth month of the old Roman calendar.
The name comes from the Latin *novem,* meaning "nine."

BIRTHSTONE *Topaz*

SUNDAY
November 1

Rescuers in Newport News, Virginia, use ropes to pull a large whale trapped on a sandbar out to sea.

MONDAY
November 2

Wildlife officials in Seattle, Washington, are trying anything to scare away the sea lions that are eating the fish—they've even tried playing loud rock music!

TUESDAY
November 3

The world's largest uncut black opal is found at Lightning Ridge in Australia. It weighs 2,020 carats and measures 4 by 2⅝ by 2½ inches. It is named Halley's Comet.

WEDNESDAY
November 4

A 22-pound, 40-year-old lobster named Monster Mike is set free in the Atlantic Ocean today. An Alaskan doctor took pity on it and paid to have it brought from Anchorage, Alaska, to Portland, Maine—by plane.

THURSDAY
November 5
Full Moon

After 2½ years, 21-year-old Tania Aebi of New York City returns home after sailing 27,000 miles around the world solo. She's the first woman and the youngest person to do it.

FRIDAY
November 6

Noboru Takeshita is elected to replace Yasuhiro Nakasone as premier of Japan. • The United Nations opens its secret files of World War II war criminals.

SATURDAY
November 7

A parade is held in Moscow's Red Square, marking the 70th anniversary of the Russian Revolution.

FUN FACT '87

There are 2,500,000 wild turkeys in the U.S.

WHO ELSE WAS BORN IN NOVEMBER?
SIR WINSTON CHURCHILL

British statesman, author
He was prime minister of England during World War II and one of the major political leaders of the time.
BORN November 30, 1874, in Blenheim Palace in Woodstock, England

SUNDAY
November 8

Jon Whitaker of England, on his horse Next Milton, wins the $50,000 Big Apple Grand Prix, an international jumping competition at the National Horse Show in New York City.

MONDAY
November 9

TERRORISM: Bomb explodes in Northern Ireland.
• A bomb also explodes in Sri Lanka.

TUESDAY
November 10

In New York City, Vincent van Gogh's *Irises* sells for an incredible $53,900,000—the highest price ever paid for a painting sold at auction.

WEDNESDAY
November 11

Veteran's Day • Roger Clemens, a pitcher for the Boston Red Sox, wins the American League Cy Young Award for the 2d year in a row.

THURSDAY
November 12

30,000,000-year-old fossils of a seabird with a wingspan of more than 18 feet have been discovered in South Carolina. It's the largest known seabird.

FRIDAY
November 13

40 Jalak Bali birds are flown from Los Angeles to the Surabaja Zoo on the Indonesian island of Java, in an effort to replenish the birds in their native habitat.

SATURDAY
November 14

10 Kemp's ridley turtles—the most endangered of all sea turtles—have washed ashore on beaches on Cape Cod in Massachusetts. Only 580 of the turtles are known to exist in the world.

SUNDAY
November 15

Tornadoes flatten homes and buildings throughout eastern Texas.

MONDAY
November 16

Colombian drug lord Carlos Rivas Lehder goes on trial in Florida.

FRIDAY THE 13TH

November 13 is the 3d Friday the 13th of 1987! The others are February 13 and March 13. Many people believe that Friday the 13th is an unlucky day, but others think just the opposite.

On November 13, 1987, members of the Friday the 13th Club in Philadelphia, Pennsylvania, celebrate with a banquet of fried grasshoppers and roasted caterpillars. Afterward, they spill salt, open umbrellas, and walk under ladders!

TUESDAY *November 17*	Baseball's George Bell of the Toronto Blue Jays is named the American League's Most Valuable Player. • A major earthquake (7.0 on the Richter scale) jolts the Gulf of Alaska.
WEDNESDAY *November 18*	Andre Dawson of the Chicago Cubs is named the National League's Most Valuable Player.
THURSDAY *November 19*	According to the National Science Foundation, an iceberg twice the size of Rhode Island has broken off from Antarctica into Ross Sea!
FRIDAY *November 20*	5-year-old Melodie Nakachian is rescued from kidnappers in Costa del Sol, Spain, when police storm the hideout.
SATURDAY *November 21*	At Christie's in New York City, a record $242,000 is paid for a stained-glass window.

SUNDAY
November 22

More than 1,000 Cuban inmates take over a prison in Oakdale, Louisiana, when they hear they may be deported.

MONDAY
November 23

Strong earthquake (6.0 on the Richter scale) hits Southern California and parts of Arizona and Nevada.

TUESDAY
November 24

Another earthquake shakes the Los Angeles area—this one measuring 6.3 on the Richter scale!

WEDNESDAY
November 25

A typhoon with winds of up to 120 miles an hour strikes the Philippines.

THURSDAY
November 26

Thanksgiving Day • 5 brothers and sisters are reunited in Fremont, California, after being separated for 58 years; they discover they all like jigsaw puzzles.

FRIDAY
November 27

American astronomers have found evidence of a large object orbiting a star 50 light-years from earth. They believe it to be a brown dwarf, which is half star, half planet.

SATURDAY
November 28

A South African jetliner crashes into the Indian Ocean.

SUNDAY
November 29

The presidential election in Haiti—the first free election in 30 years—is canceled because of an outbreak of violence.

MONDAY
November 30

Archaeologists report that they have found gold, silver, ivory, ebony, and ostrich eggs in a shipwreck discovered off the coast of Turkey. The treasure is from the time of King Tutankhamen of Egypt, 3,300 years ago!

CARVING OF WINGED HORSE WINS ICE-CARVING CHAMPIONSHIP

U.S. SOLAR-POWERED SUNRAYCER WINS RACE ACROSS AUSTRALIA

PRESIDENT OF TUNISIA OVERTHROWN
STATE OF EMERGENCY DECLARED IN BANGLADESH

December

December used to be the tenth month of the year (the Latin *decem* means "ten"). The old Roman calendar began with March.

BIRTHSTONE *Turquoise*

TUESDAY
December 1

The first manned hydrogen-balloon voyage was made on December 1, 1783.

WEDNESDAY
December 2

SPACE NEWS: NASA announces that it will launch an unmanned spacecraft to Jupiter in 1989.

THURSDAY
December 3

The roseate tern has been declared an endangered species by the U.S. Fish and Wildlife Service.

FRIDAY
December 4

A 72-page manuscript by Albert Einstein, explaining his theory of relativity, has been sold for the record price of $1,160,000!

SATURDAY
December 5

Full Moon

Tinsel Day • The Bradford comet is visible in parts of Europe.

SUNDAY
December 6

More than 200,000 protesters march on Washington, D.C., for human rights in the Soviet Union and for the right of Soviet Jews to emigrate.

MONDAY
December 7

A Pacific Southwest Airlines jet crashes near Paso Robles, California. Officials suspect the crash to be the work of a former employee.

TUESDAY
December 8

In Washington, D.C., President Reagan and Soviet leader Gorbachev sign a treaty agreeing to get rid of all medium-range nuclear weapons.

WEDNESDAY
December 9

Nancy Reagan gives Raisa Gorbachev a personal tour of the White House.

WHO ELSE WAS BORN IN DECEMBER?
LARRY BIRD

U.S. basketball player
He was voted Most Valuable Player 3 times in a
row by the National Basketball Association and
has played for the Boston Celtics since 1980.
BORN December 7, 1956, in West Baden, Indiana

THURSDAY
December 10

Officials in Ravenna, Italy, announce that a fantasy amusement
park like Disneyland is going to be built outside their city.

FRIDAY
December 11

European astronomers are given the
go-ahead for the world's largest
telescope; it will take 10 years to build
and will be called the VLT (Very
Large Telescope).

SATURDAY
December 12

A scientist at the Goddard Space Flight Center in Maryland has
invented a transmitter that is small enough to be swallowed!

SUNDAY
December 13

The Detroit Pistons beat the Denver Nuggets, 186–184,
in a game with the highest point total in professional
basketball history. 3 overtimes are needed.

MONDAY
December 14

WEATHER HISTORY: On this day in 1924, the
temperature dropped 79 degrees in Helena, Montana.

TUESDAY
December 15

Hanukkah begins at sunset. • Happy birthday to
Nero, the Roman emperor, who was born in A.D. 37.

WEDNESDAY
December 16

The longest and the largest Mafia trial in Italian
history ends in Sicily; 338 out of 452 on trial are
convicted. The trial began on February 10, 1986!

HEY, how
about a
pizza?!

FUN FACT '87

So far, 100,000,000,000,000,000,000,000,000,000,000,000
snowflakes have fallen on earth

THURSDAY
December 17

A strong earthquake rocks Tokyo in Japan; it registers 6.6 on the Richter scale. • The secretary-general of the Czechoslovakian Communist Party resigns.

FRIDAY
December 18

In 1865, the 13th amendment to the Constitution, prohibiting slavery, was ratified.

SATURDAY
December 19

10 Japanese spider crabs, which have a leg span of up to 10 feet, are sent to the National Zoological Park in Washington, D.C., from Japan.

SUNDAY
December 20

A passenger ferry carrying 1,500 people crashes into an oil tanker south of Manila; both ships sink!

MONDAY
December 21

50 years ago, the Walt Disney movie *Snow White and the Seven Dwarfs* first opened. • Members of the environmental group Greenpeace tow a 50-foot-long plastic humpback whale across the bow of a whaling ship docked at Yokohama, Japan, to protest the killing of whales.

TUESDAY
December 22

Winter solstice • A North American bald eagle that was blown across the Atlantic Ocean to Ireland by strong winds is flown back to New York by jet—first-class!

WEDNESDAY
December 23

Cosmonauts Vladimir Georgeyevich Titov and Musa Khiramanovich Manarov in the *Soyuz TM-4* dock with the *Mir* space station to replace the *Mir* crew.

THURSDAY
December 24

Christmas Eve • In Port Charlotte, Florida, a 12-year-old girl survives an alligator attack by grabbing its jaws after it grabs her legs.

TINSEL TOWNS

Some people like to celebrate Christmas all year round. 89 cities and towns in the U.S. have the word *Christmas* in their names. 29 have the word Noel in them. Arizona, Georgia, and Indiana all have towns named Santa Claus. There is even a place called Wreath in Wyoming!

HOTTEST CHRISTMAS TOYS OF 1987

The Real Ghostbusters,
including the ghost zapper and a proton pack
Pictionary
Nintendo games
Captain Power jets

FRIDAY
December 25

Christmas • 33,300,000 Christmas trees have been sold this year, according to the National Christmas Tree Association.

SATURDAY
December 26

COOL!

Alfred B. Levine has invented a dual electronic camera—it takes 2 pictures at once!

SUNDAY
December 27

In North Brunswick, New Jersey, 100 factory workers have been suspended for coming to work wearing Santa Claus hats.

MONDAY
December 28

In London, England, the statue of Winston Churchill is lit up for the first time.

TUESDAY
December 29

Yuri Romanenko returns to earth in a space capsule, after having spent a record 326 days in space. He is a little taller than when he left!

WEDNESDAY
December 30

Ed Boyajian is named World Champion Liar in Burlington, Wisconsin. The winning lie: He said that he had played one side of a record for so long, he could hear both sides at the same time.

THURSDAY
December 31

New Year's Eve • At exactly 11:59 P.M., a second is added to the world's clocks to make up for the slowing of the earth's rotation.

1,600 KILLED WHEN PHILIPPINE FERRY COLLIDES WITH OIL TANKER OFF MANILA

METROPOLITAN MUSEUM OF ART GETS $10,000,000 GIFT

338 ITALIANS CONVICTED IN LARGEST MAFIA TRIAL

ARABS PROTEST IN ISRAEL

YOUR YEAR AT A GLANCE

A lot happened the year you were born. How many events shown on the cover can you identify? Turn the page upside down for the answers.

1. Top ten baby names in 1987 (See June)   2. Sharks lose teeth every time they bite something! (See June Fun Fact)   3. Ohio man returns home from walk around the world (April 1)   4. Members of the Friday the 13th Club celebrate with a special feast (November 13)   5. Soviets send two monkeys up in space (September 29)   6. Cowboys herd 400 buffalo to their summer home (March 23)   7. 12-year-old girl survives an alligator attack in Port Charlotte, Florida (December 24)   8. Archaeologists in China find 1,700 terra-cotta warriors and horses buried in an imperial tomb (July 13)   9. Mountain climber falls 1,500 feet down Mount McKinley (June 7)